HEAVEN VISIONS

EYE WITNESSES OF PEOPLE WHO VISITED HEAVEN AND RETURNED.

AJAY MALHOTRA

Made with ♥ on the Notion Press Platform
www.notionpress.com

HEAVEN VISIONS

EYE WITNESSES OF PEOPLE WHO VISITED HEAVEN AND RETURNED.

FOR THE GLORY OF GOD AND FOR THE BENEFIT OF MEN

VERY SIMPLE TO READ AND UNDERSTAND.

Jesus said, Let not your heart be troubled; you believe in God, believe also in Me. In My Father's house are many mansions; if it were not so, I would have told you. I go to prepare a place for you

TABLE OF CONTENTS:

· MANSIONS

Jesus said,

Let not your heart be troubled; you believe in God, believe also in Me. In My Father's house are many mansions; if it were not so, I would have told you. I go to prepare a place for you

Very tall angels were standing outside the gate. Both of them wore glistening robes and had swords in their hands. Their hair was like spun gold, and their faces gleamed with light. Their wings had eyes.

Welcome theme: "Come and see the glory of your God."

MUSIC:

Music filled the whole atmosphere. All creatures sing praises to God. Even animals, birds, flowers and trees sing praises.

Flowers turn and face wherever Jesus goes.

Wave after powerful wave of beautiful music and singing surged across the landscape and seemed to envelop everything and everyone.

All kinds of food like on earth are available, except meat. Only fruits, veggies, even ice cream.

People in heaven work in professions that they did on earth- cooking/restaurants, carpentry, building mansions, teaching, painting, etc, but no hospitals.

All enjoyment/amusement parks are available. Even movie theatres are there. Only clean movies. No bad language or nudity.

No marriages and no sexual enjoyment. No gender. No genitals for people. No sweat/urine/bowel movement.

Diamonds-glittering, glistening, exquisite diamonds-diamonds everywhere! Some were as large as blocks of concrete. Some of these diamonds seemed to be for the mansions of those who were soul winners on Earth. It seemed that every time someone led a soul to Christ, heaven provided a diamond for that faithful Christian.

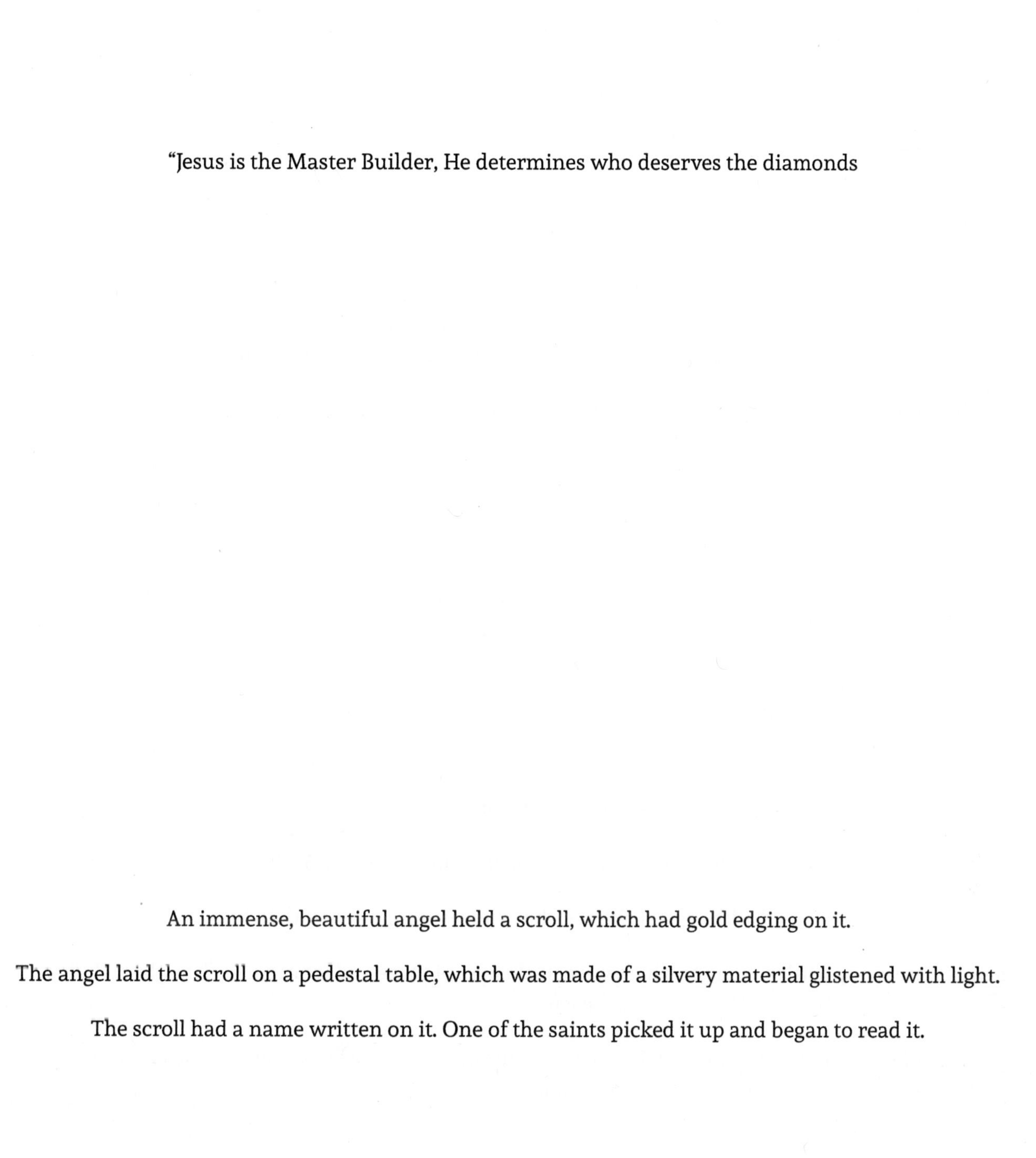

“Jesus is the Master Builder, He determines who deserves the diamonds

An immense, beautiful angel held a scroll, which had gold edging on it.

The angel laid the scroll on a pedestal table, which was made of a silvery material glistened with light.

The scroll had a name written on it. One of the saints picked it up and began to read it.

They go. This scroll I hold is a report from earth of a person who has led someone to Jesus, who fed the poor, who Clothed the naked-who did great things for God."

God has prepared the city, and Jesus is preparing a place there for those of us who love Him.

The room of tears:

The angels catch our tears and put them in bottles (Psalm 56:8).

The room Lined with crystal shelves, the inside walls glowed with light.

On the shelves were many bottles, some of which were in clusters of three and looked like clear glass. Under each

Sparkling cluster of glass-like bottles was a plaque with a name on it. There were many of these bottles in the Room.

Inside the room a man who appeared to have been glorified. His deep purple robe was very beautiful and looked like velvet.

An elegant table, which was made of a rich-looking material and glowed with majestic splendor, was just inside the door.

Books were lying on the table, and they looked as if they were sown in the most beautiful silk-like material

Some had diamonds, pearls, and lace on them; others had green and purple stones on them.

All of them were intricately made.

Alargeangelthebeautyandmajestyofthisheavenly being:

He wore a white, glistening garment with gold-edged trim that went all the way down at the front. He seemed to be about twelve feet tall and had very large wings.

He has just brought a bowl of tears from the earth.

The angel handed him the bowl, along with a piece of paper. The note held the name of the person whosc tears were in the bowl.

The man in the room read the note and then went over to one of the places where the bottles were kept. He read the Plaque under the bottle, and it matched the person from earth who was named in the note.

The man picked up the bottle that was nearly full and brought it over to the bowl. He poured the tears from the Golden bowl into the bottle.

Then the man poured a drop from the bottle, one little teardrop, on the first page of the book. When he did, words began to appear immediately. Beautiful words, elegantly handwritten, started appearing on the page.

Each time a tear fell on a page, a whole page of writing appeared. He continued doing this page after page, time and time again.

"The most perfect prayers are those that are bathed in tears that come from the hearts and souls of men and women on earth."

O a huge place with thousands and thousands of people and heavenly beings. People seemed to fade away, and an even greater display of God's glory began to appear everywhere. The high praises of God became thunderous.

The throne of God.

A huge cloud, a mist, and image of the Being in the cloud. Glory of God and a rainbow were over the throne.

Many horses with riders were beside the throne.

A book was lying on the huge altar in front of God's throne. Angels bowing before Him

A man's hand come out of the cloud and opens up the book

The most beautiful perfume filled the whole area

It was the hand of God that opened the book as smoke ascending from the book

The book contains the prayers of the saints and God was sending His angels to earth to answer the prayers from the cries of their hearts. Everybody was Praising and magnifying God.

As God opened up the book, pages began to come out of the volume and fly into the hands of the angels on the Horses shouting and saying, "Go, answer her prayers! Go, Answer his prayers!"

Glory to God, heaven is a real place! We will really be going there. And, we will not be vapors of smoke floating on a cloud when we go to heaven.

One of the wonderful things about heaven is that our tears and sorrows will be replaced with eternal joy, as Promised in the Word of God. Yet, there is much more!

Heaven is a real place. It is a literal destination. It is not some ephemeral dream, some imagined vision.

God has revealed to all of us many of the realities of heaven through the Holy Scriptures.

THE FIRST HEAVEN

First, there is an atmospheric heaven. This is the atmosphere around the earth. It is where the birds fly and the

Winds blow. This is where showers, storms, mists, vapors, and clouds are formed.

The sky is the place the angel was referring to in Acts 1:11 when he asked the disciples why they were "gazing up into heaven." Jesus, when He

Was talking to His Father, "lifted up His eyes to heaven" (John 17:1), or toward the sky.

THESECONDHEAVEN

Then, there is the heaven of space. This is the region of the sun, the moon, and the stars

THETHIRDHEAVEN

The destination of the righteous, however, is beyond the atmosphere and the starry skies. This place is what the

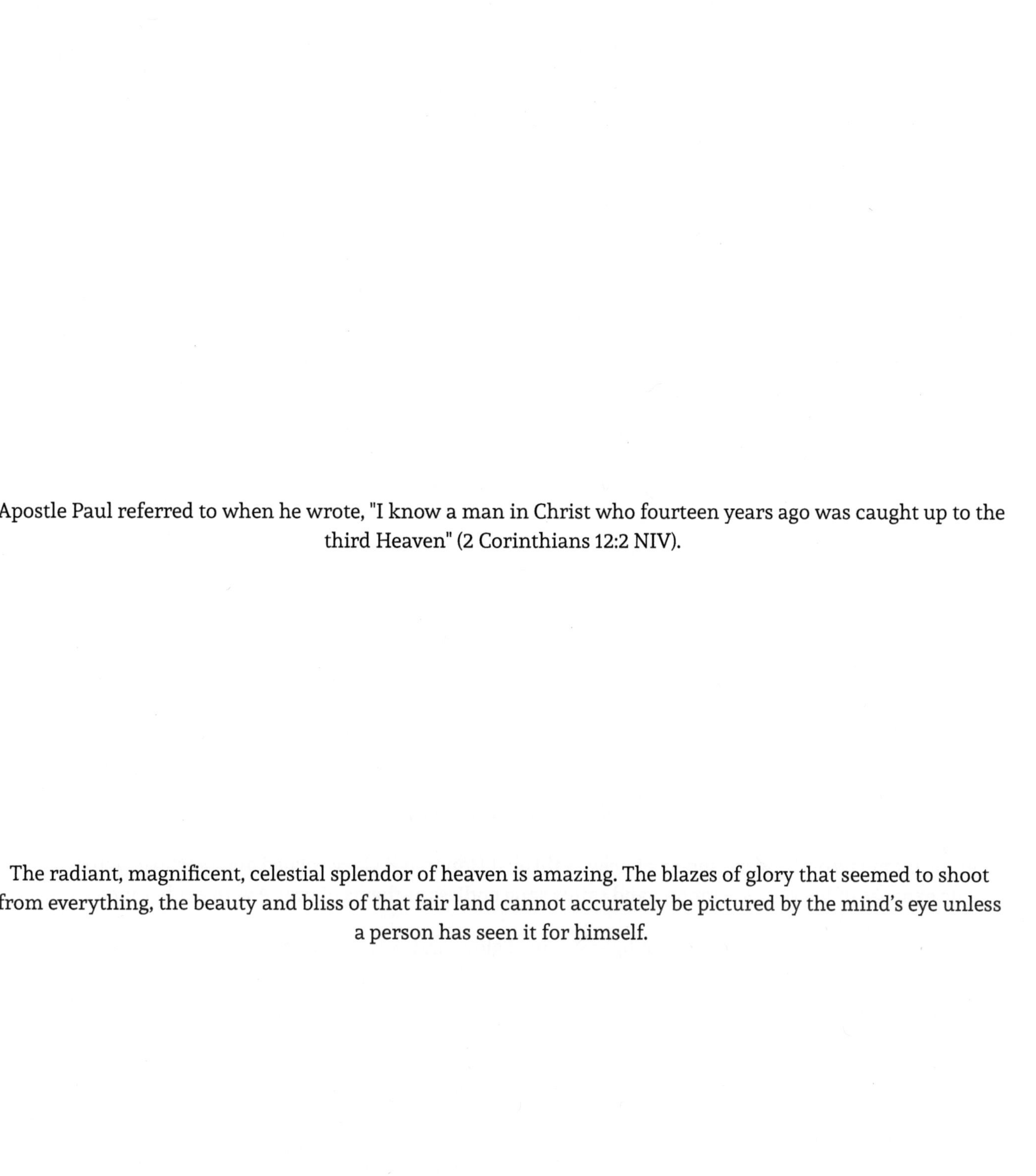

Apostle Paul referred to when he wrote, "I know a man in Christ who fourteen years ago was caught up to the third Heaven" (2 Corinthians 12:2 NIV).

The radiant, magnificent, celestial splendor of heaven is amazing. The blazes of glory that seemed to shoot from everything, the beauty and bliss of that fair land cannot accurately be pictured by the mind's eye unless a person has seen it for himself.

Joy, peace, and happiness everywhere

The magnificent music of the worshippers of heaven thrilled Honor and glory echoed and reechoed across the wide expanse of heaven as seraphim and saints sang endless anthems of praise with exuberance.

Varied colors of radiant light signified glory and power. Blazes of

Splendor flashed from the throne. Beams of glory radiated from it. So much of heaven seems transparent, and those illustrious beams that come forth from the throne are filled with light that is reflected in every part of paradise!

COLURS MORE THAN VIBGYOR ARE PRESENT.

You will find colors that are not here on earth. More than those found in a rainbow. VIBGYOR. New colours not found on earth/

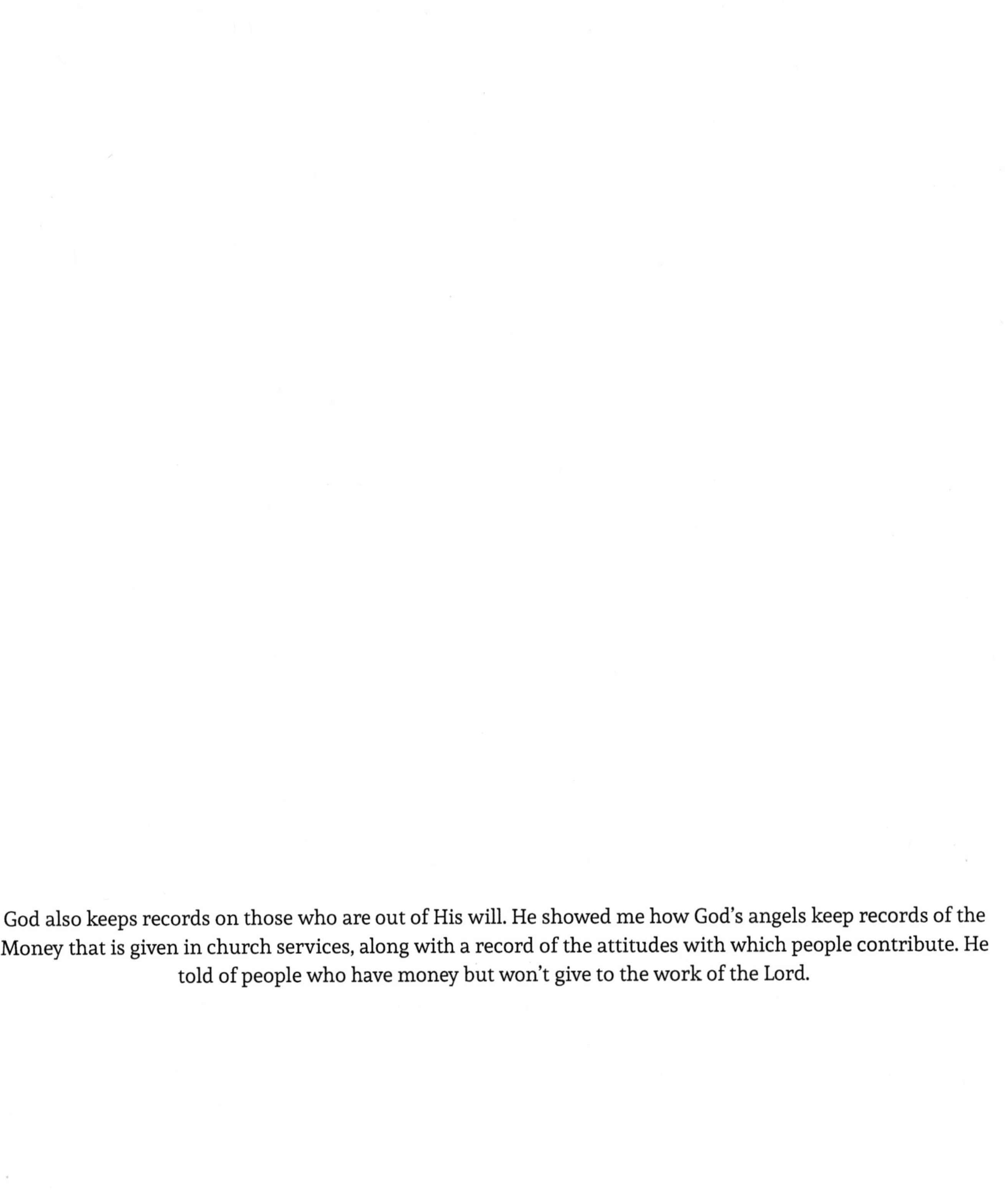

God also keeps records on those who are out of His will. He showed me how God's angels keep records of the Money that is given in church services, along with a record of the attitudes with which people contribute. He told of people who have money but won't give to the work of the Lord.

Horses looked as noble as marble chess pieces. They looked as if they were huge statues that had been chiseled out of boulders, but they were real and alive. Their hooves were gigantic. They were pure white and very regal.

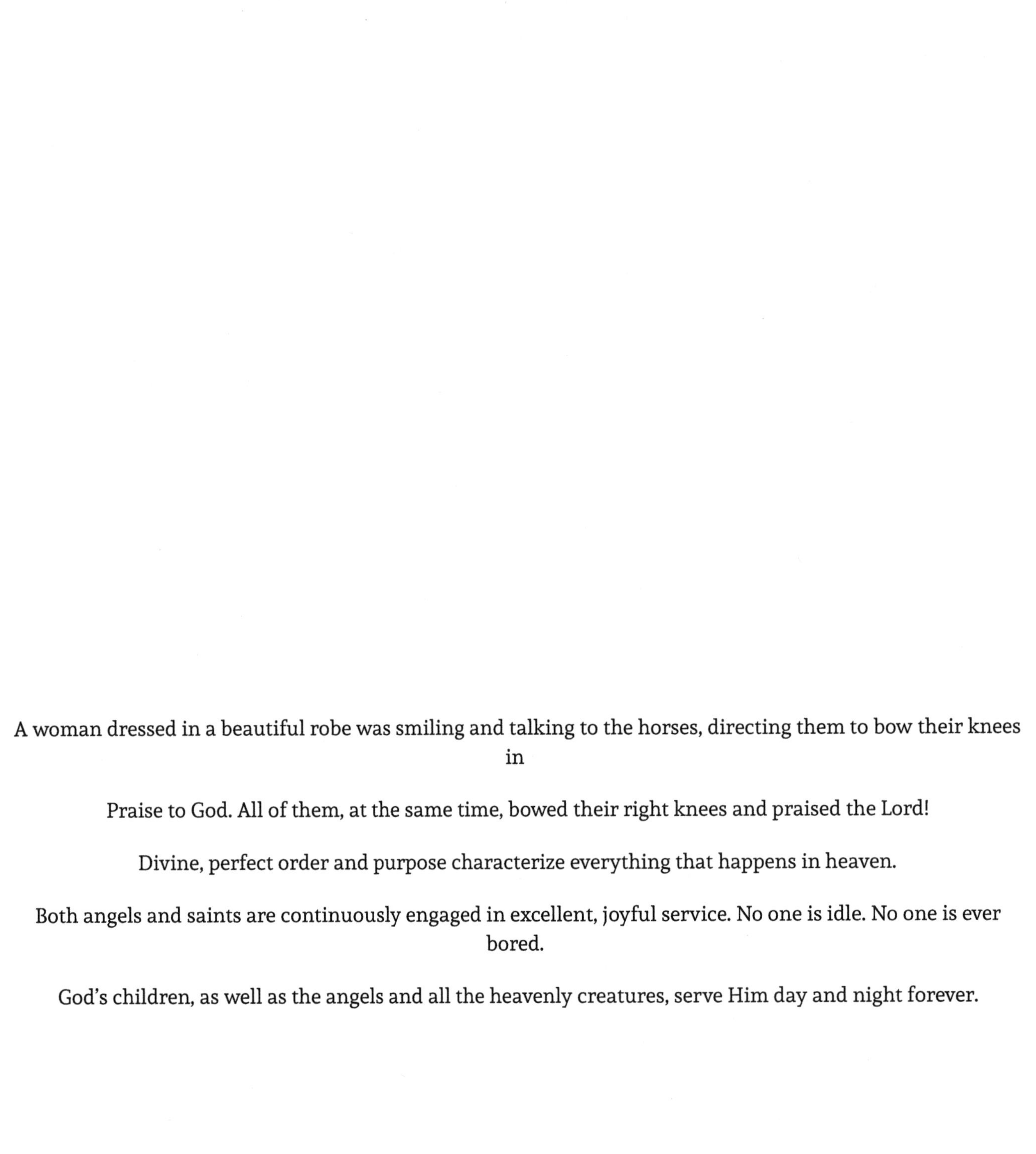

A woman dressed in a beautiful robe was smiling and talking to the horses, directing them to bow their knees in

Praise to God. All of them, at the same time, bowed their right knees and praised the Lord!

Divine, perfect order and purpose characterize everything that happens in heaven.

Both angels and saints are continuously engaged in excellent, joyful service. No one is idle. No one is ever bored.

God's children, as well as the angels and all the heavenly creatures, serve Him day and night forever.

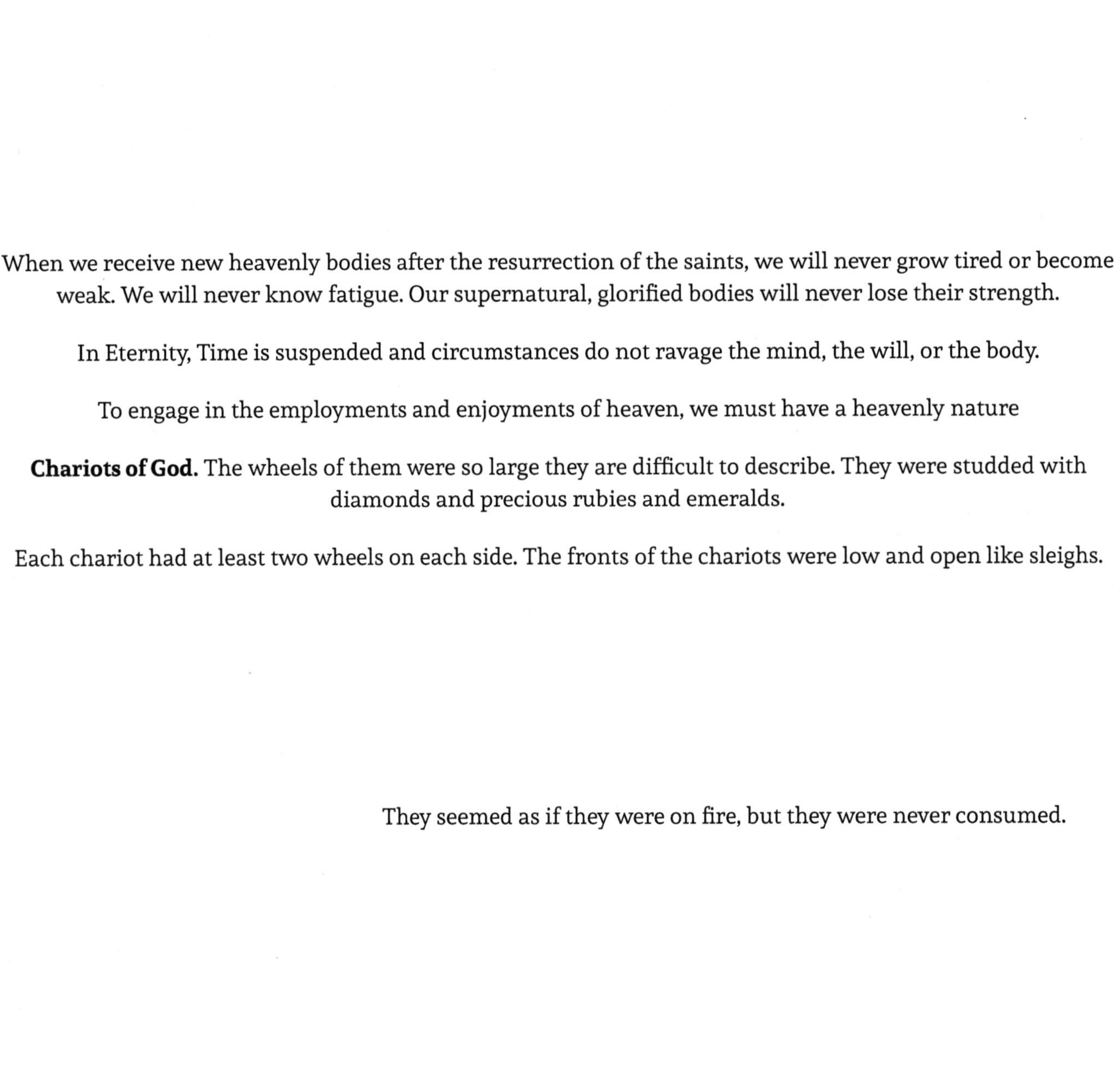

When we receive new heavenly bodies after the resurrection of the saints, we will never grow tired or become weak. We will never know fatigue. Our supernatural, glorified bodies will never lose their strength.

In Eternity, Time is suspended and circumstances do not ravage the mind, the will, or the body.

To engage in the employments and enjoyments of heaven, we must have a heavenly nature

Chariots of God. The wheels of them were so large they are difficult to describe. They were studded with diamonds and precious rubies and emeralds.

Each chariot had at least two wheels on each side. The fronts of the chariots were low and open like sleighs.

They seemed as if they were on fire, but they were never consumed.

“Those who had been dismembered, paralyzed, crippled, or had died prematurely were now in a state of perfection. They had been made whole!

In heaven, you will know everyone. You will know Abraham, Isaac, and Jacob. You will know Moses and all the prophets. You will know all the disciples of the New Testament.

You will know every person in heaven. You will know just as God knows you (1 Corinthians 13:12). You will have very extensive knowledge

The most beautiful clouds were billowing in and out around the throne. Shaped almost like the mushroom cloud of an atomic explosion, each cloud was mixed with glory and beautiful colors.

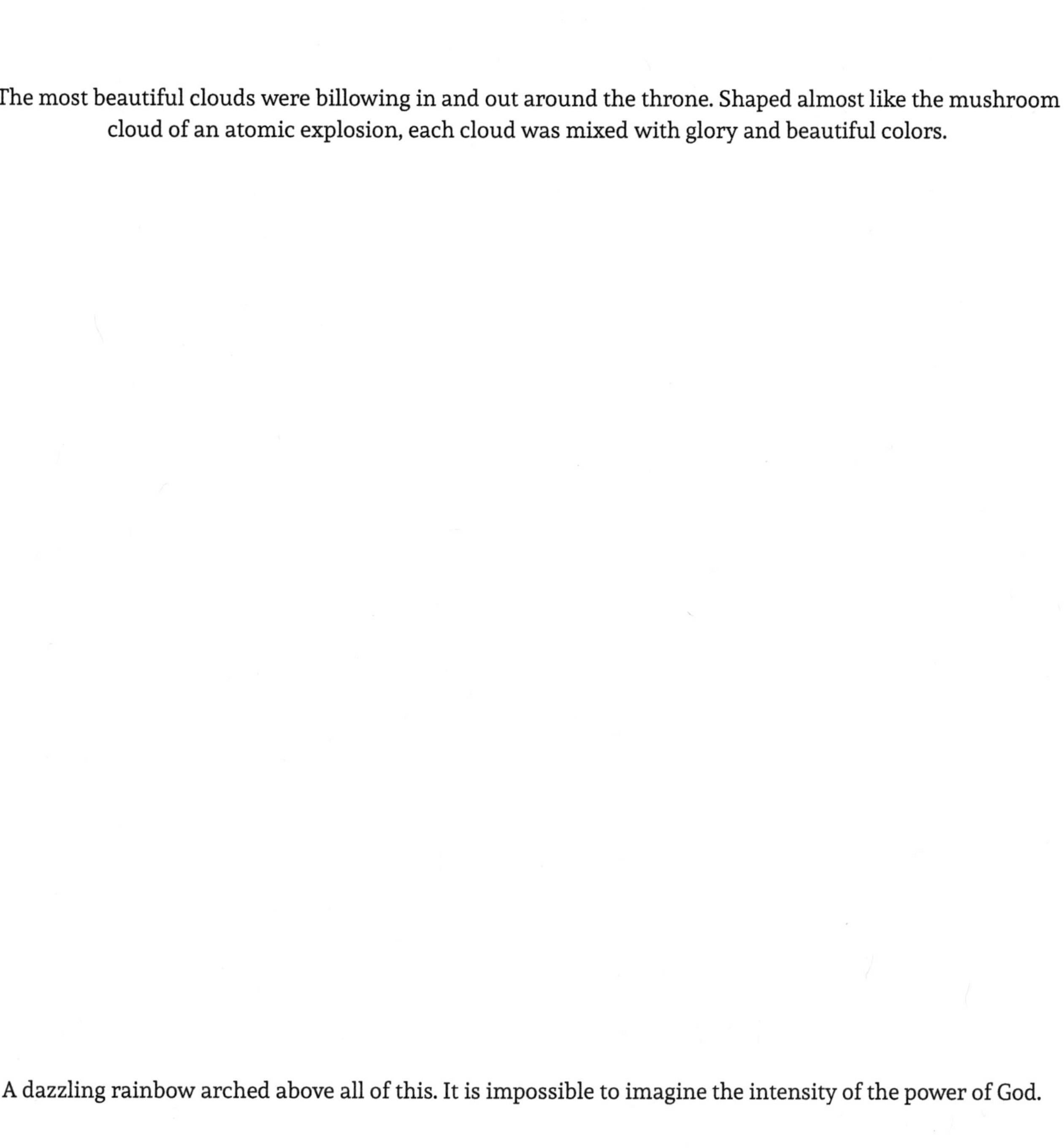

A dazzling rainbow arched above all of this. It is impossible to imagine the intensity of the power of God.

The River of Life flowed forth from the throne of God. It was like a sea of glass, like a sea of crystal, but it was flowing.

The big, white, magnificent horses looked as though they were made out of marble. They were beautiful and without a single flaw in any of them. They were elegant, like chess

Pieces, but they were physically real. The white blankets on the horses' backs were neatly trimmed with gold edging. Golden reins were in their mouths. They had ornaments on their feet and even on the brush of their tails. These horses

stood alert before the throne.

Twelve angels standing before the throne had trumpets and musical horns by their sides. Their flowing, glowing garments were trimmed with gold and embedded with big rubies and all kinds of immense stones.

Many musical instruments were present. They were the most spectacular instruments you could ever imagine seeing. Oh, the beauty of heaven! There were many harps.

RECEPTION OF NEW SOULS:

When new souls come to heaven, angels meet them and lead them immediately through the River of Life. The angels escort the new souls to a place where other angels outfit them with gowns of salvation, which are robes of righteousness. Then the angelic guides take them to the room of crowns, where each person is fitted with a crown.

Relatives and family members and friends greet the new soul at the entrance gates of heaven. Just as we receive our family at airport with hugs and kisses and greetings.

All of these things are done in beautiful, perfect order. The angels are perfectly happy while doing them.

TV LIKE SCREEN:

Souls in heaven watch their loved ones on earth through a big screen in a special room. If their loved ones on earth are having a gathering or a celebration, angels will tell them to o the screen room and the souls will watch on the screen what's happening on earth with their loved ones.

MANSIONS:

There are mansions as big as a city. Some are built on mountains, some suspend in the air and some are on the ground.

The buildings sway with the music of worship.

RIVER

The river from the throne of God splits out into smaller canals and flows into every mansion or house in the heaven. Jesus is present at every place. He sometime dines and eats with the families in the mansions/houses.

DAY AND NIGHT TIMES:

Day time is full of light from the throne. Lights of different intensities are found. Dim light, bright light, dazzling light, and heavy light. But it is pleasing and does not hurt.

TO BE IN HEAVEN YOU MUST SAY THIS SIMPLE PRAYER:

"LORD JESUS I ACCEPT YOU AS MY LORD AND SAVIOUR. COME INO MY HEART. LIVE IN ME AND FORGIVE MY SINS. THANK YOU HESUS."

AND YOU MUST FORGIVE YOUR ENEMIES. PUNISH AND FORGIVE THEM. TAKE COMPENSATION FROM YOUR ENEMIES AND FORGIVE THEM.

MORE INFORMATION ABOUT HEAVEN WILL COME IN MY NEXT EBOOK.

TILL THEN PLEASE ENJOY. BYE FOR NOW.

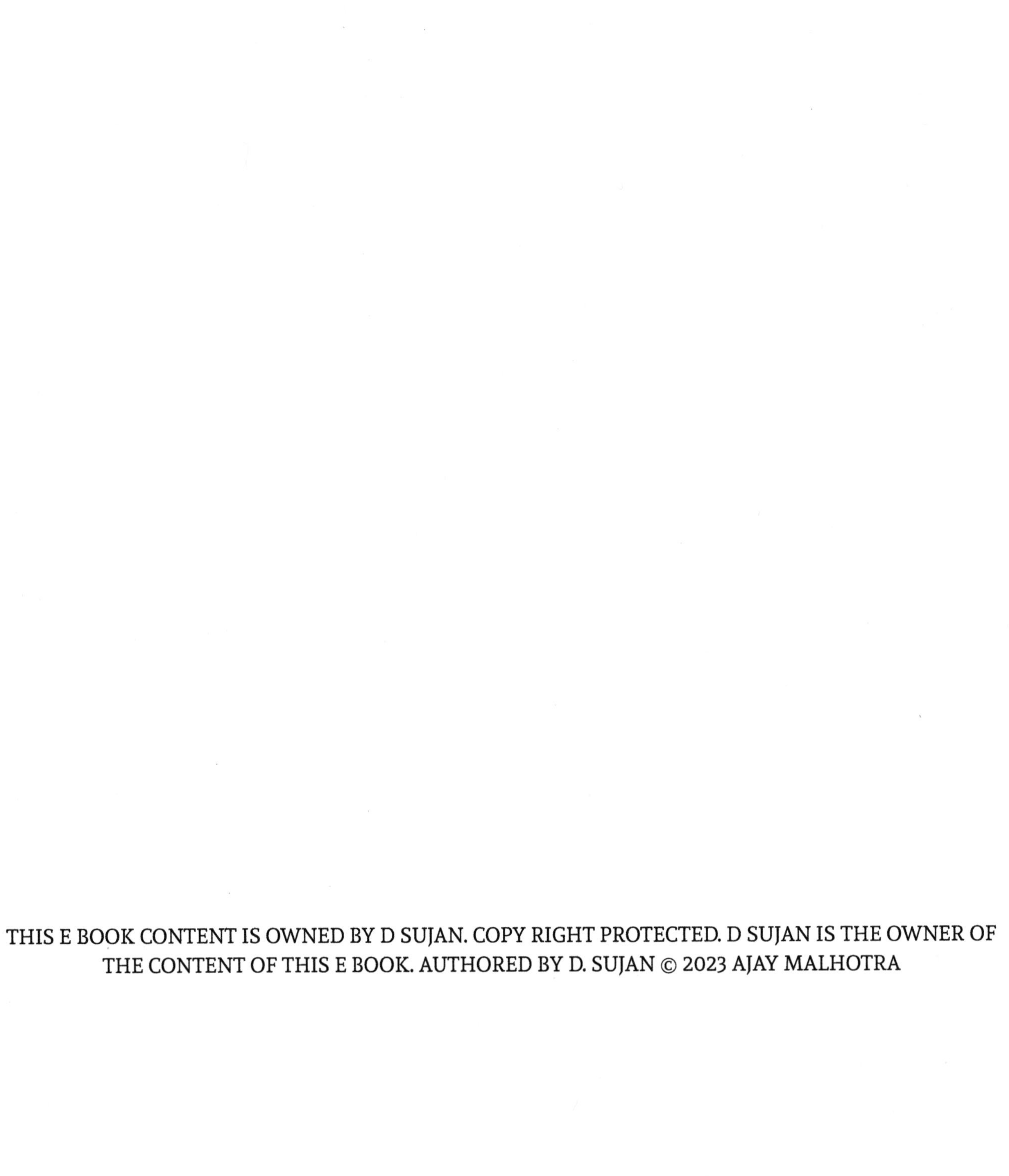

Contents

Foreword

Printed by Libri Plureos GmbH in Hamburg,
Germany